I0172810

It Works

R.H. JARRETT

&

Self-Mastery Through
Conscious Autosuggestion

EMILE COUE

It Works

R.H. JARRETT

The Famous Little Red Book That Makes Your Dreams Come True.

A clear, definite, common sense plan of accomplishment.

The author sent the manuscript of this book for criticism to a friend, who returned it with the notation: *it works.*

This judgment born of experience was adopted as the title of the book.

A concise, definite, resultful plan with rules, explanations and suggestions for bettering your condition in life.

If you KNOW what you WANT, you can HAVE IT

The man who wrote this book is highly successful and widely known for his generosity and helpful spirit. He gives full credit for all that he has accomplished in mastering circumstances, accumulating wealth, and wining friends to the silent working out of the simple, powerful truth which he tells of in his work. He shows you here an easy, open road to a larger, happier life.

Knowing that the greatest good comes from helping others without expecting praise, the author of this work has requested that his name be omitted.

It Works

What is the real secret of obtaining desirable possessions? Are some people born under a lucky star or other charm which enables them to have all that which seems so desirable, and if not, what is the cause of the difference in conditions under which men live?

Many years ago, feeling that there must be a logical answer to this question, I decided to find out, if possible, what it was. I found the answer to my own satisfaction, and for years, have given the information to others who have used it successfully.

From a scientific, psychological or theological viewpoint, some of the following statements may be interpreted as incorrect, but nevertheless, the plan has brought the results desired to those who have followed the simple instructions, and it is my sincere belief that I am now presenting it in a way which will bring happiness and possessions to many more.

If wishes were horses, beggars would ride, is the attitude taken by the average man and woman in regard to possessions. They are not aware of a power so near that it is overlooked; so simple in operation that it is difficult to conceive; and so sure in results that it is not made use of consciously, or recognized as the cause of failure or success.

"Gee, I wish that were mine" is the outburst of Jimmy, the office boy, as a new red roadster goes by; and Florence, the telephone operator, expresses the same thought regarding a ring in the jeweler's window; while poor old Jones, the bookkeeper, during the Sunday stroll, replies to his wife, "Yes, dear, it would be nice to have a home like that, but it is out of the question. We will have to continue to rent." Landem, the salesman, protests that he does all the work, gets the short end of the money and will some day quit his job and find a real one, and President Bondum, in his private sanctorum, voices a bitter tirade against the annual attack of hay fever. At home it is much the same. Last evening, father declared that daughter Mabel was headed straight for disaster, and today, mother's allowance problem and other trying affairs fade into insignificance as she exclaims, "This is the last straw. Robert's schoolteacher wants to see me this afternoon. His reports are terrible, I know, but I'm late for Bridge now. She'll have to wait until tomorrow."

So goes the endless stream of expressions like these from millions of people in all classes who give no thought to what they really want, and who are getting all they are entitled to or expect. If you are of these millions of thoughtless talkers or wishers and would like a decided change from your present condition, you can have it; but first of all you must know what you want and this is no easy task. When you can train your objective mind (the mind you use every day) to decide definitely upon the things or conditions you desire, you will have taken your first big step in accomplishing or securing what you know you want.

To get what you want is no more mysterious or uncertain than the radio waves all around you. Tune in correctly and you get a perfect result, but to do this, it is, of course, necessary to know something of your equipment and have a plan of operation.

You have within you a mighty power, anxious and willing to serve you, a power capable of giving you that which you earnestly desire. This power is described by Thomson Jay Hudson, Ph.D., LL.D., author of *The Law of Psychic Phenomena,* as your subjective mind. Other learned writers use different names and terms, but all agree that it is omnipotent. Therefore, I call this Power, God.

Regardless of the name of the Great Power, or the conscious admission of a God, the Power is capable and willing to carry to a complete and perfect conclusion very earnest desire of your objective mind, but you must be really in earnest about what you want.

Occasional wishing or halfhearted wanting does not form a perfect connection or communication with your omnipotent power. You must be in earnest, sincerely and truthfully desiring certain conditions or things, mental, physical or spiritual.

Your objective mind and will are so vacillating that you usually only WISH for things and the wonderful, capable power within you does not function. Most wishes are simply vocal expressions.

Jimmy, the office boy, gave no thought of possessing the red roadster. Landem, the salesman, was not thinking of any other job or even thinking at all. President Bondum knew he had hay fever and was expecting it. Father's business was quite successful and mother no doubt brought home first prize from the Bridge party that day, but they had no fixed idea of what they really wanted their children to accomplish and were actually helping to bring about the unhappy conditions which existed.

If you are in earnest about changing you present condition, here is a concise, definite, resultful plan, with rules, explanations and suggestions.

THE PLAN

Write down on paper in order of their importance the things and conditions you really want. Do not be afraid of wanting too much. Go the limit in writing down your wants. Change the list daily, adding to or taking from it, until you have it about right. Do not be discouraged on account of changes, as this is natural.

There will always be changes and additions with accomplishments and increasing desires.

THREE POSITIVE RULES OF ACCOMPLISHMENT

1   Read the list of what you want three times each day: morning, noon and night.

2   Think of what you want as often as possible.

3   Do not talk to anyone about your plan except to the Great Power within you, which will unfold to your Objective Mind the method of accomplishment

It is obvious that you cannot acquire faith at the start. Some of your desires, from all practical reasoning, may seem positively unattainable; but, nevertheless, write them down on your list in their proper place of importance to you. There is no need to analyze how this Power within you is going to accomplish your desires. Such a procedure is as unnecessary as trying to figure out why a grain of corn placed in fertile soil shoots up a green stalk, blossoms, and produces an ear of corn containing hundreds of grains, each capable of doing what the one grain did. If you will follow this definite plan and carry out the three simple rules, the method of accomplishment will unfold quite as mysteriously as the ear of corn appears on the stalk, and in most cases much sooner than you expect. When new desires, deserving position at or about the top of your list, come to you, then you may rest assured you are progressing correctly.

Removing from your list items which at first you thought you wanted, is another sure indication of progress. It is natural to be skeptical and have doubts, distrust and questionings, but when these thoughts arise, get out your list. Read it over; or if you have it memorized, talk to your inner self about your desires until the doubts that interfere with your progress are gone.

Remember, nothing can prevent your having that which you earnestly desire. Others have these things. Why not you? The Omnipotent Power within you does not enter into any controversial argument. It is waiting and willing to serve when you are ready, but you objective mind is so susceptible to suggestion that it is almost impossible to make any satisfactory progress when surrounded by skeptics. Therefore, choose your friends carefully and associate with people who now have some of the things you really want, but do not discuss your method of accomplishment with them.

Put down on your list of wants such material things as money, home, automobile, or whatever it may be, but do not stop there. Be more definite. If you want an automobile, decide what kind, style, price, color, and all the other details, including when you want it. If you want a home, plan the structure, grounds and furnishings. Decide on location and cost. If you want money, write down the amount. If you want to break a record in your business, put it down. It may be a sales record. If so, write out the total, the date required, then the number of items you must sell to make it, also list your prospects and put after each name the sum expected.

This may seem very foolish at first, but you can never realize your desires if you do not know positively and in detail what you want and when you want it. If you cannot decide this, you are not in earnest. You must be definite, and when you are, results will be surprising and almost unbelievable.

A natural and ancient enemy will no doubt appear when you get your first taste of accomplishment. This enemy is Discredit, in form of such thoughts as: *It can't be possible; it just happened to be. What a remarkable coincidence!*

When such thoughts occur, give thanks and assert credit to your Omnipotent Power for the accomplishment. By doing this, you gain assurance and more accomplishment, and in time, prove to yourself that there is a law, which actually works - at all times - when you are in tune with it.

Sincere and earnest thanks cannot be given without gratitude and it is impossible to be thankful and grateful without being happy. Therefore, when you are thanking your greatest and best friend, your Omnipotent

Power, for the gifts received, do so with all your soul, and let it be reflected in your face. The Power and what it does is beyond understanding. Do not try to understand it, but accept the accomplishment with thankfulness, happiness and strengthened faith.

CAUTION

It is possible to want and obtain that which will make you miserable; that which will wreck the happiness of others; that which will cause sickness and death; that which will rob you of eternal life. You can have what you want, but you must take all that goes with it: so in planning your wants, plan that which you are sure will give to you and your fellow man the greatest good here on earth; thus paving the way to that future hope beyond the pale of human understanding.

This method of securing what you want applies to everything you are capable of desiring and the scope being so great, it is suggested that your first list consist of only those things with which you are quite familiar, such as an amount of money or accomplishment, or the possession of material things. Such desires as these are more easily and quickly obtained than the discontinuance of fixed habits, the welfare of others and the healing of mental or bodily ills. Accomplish the lesser things first. Then take the next step, and when that is accomplished, you will seek the higher and really important objectives in life, but long before you reach this stage of your progress, many worthwhile desires will find their place on your list. One will be to help others as you have been helped. Great is the reward to those who help and give without thought of self, as it is impossible to be unselfish without gain.

IN CONCLUSION

A short while ago, Dr. Emile Coue came to this country and showed thousands of people how to help themselves. Thousands of others spoofed at the idea, refused his assistance and are today where they were before his visit. So with the statements and plan presented to you now. You can reject or accept. You can remain as you are or have anything you want. The choice is yours, but God grant that you may find in this short volume the inspiration to choose aright, follow the plan and thereby obtain, as so many others have, all things, whatever they may be, that you desire. Read the entire book over again, and again, AND THEN AGAIN.

Memorize the three simple rules. Test them now on what you want most this minute. This book could have extended easily over 350 pages but it has been deliberately shortened to make it as easy as possible for you to read, understand and use. Will you try it? Thousands of bettered lives will testify to the fact that: **It Works.**

Self-Mastery Through Conscious Autosuggestion

Emile Coue

Suggestion, or rather Autosuggestion, is quite a new subject, and yet at the same time it is as old as the world. It is new in the sense that until now it has been wrongly studied and in consequence wrongly understood; it is old because it dates from the appearance of man on the earth. In fact autosuggestion is an instrument that we possess at birth, and in this instrument, or rather in this force, resides a marvelous and incalculable power, which according to circumstances produces the best or the worst results. Knowledge of this force is useful to each one of us, but it is peculiarly indispensable to doctors, magistrates, lawyers, and to those engaged in the work of education.

By knowing how to practice it consciously it is possible in the first place to avoid provoking in others bad autosuggestions which may have disastrous consequences, and secondly, consciously to provoke good ones instead, thus bringing physical health to the sick, and moral health to the neurotic and the erring - the unconscious victims of anterior autosuggestions, and to guide into the right path those who had a tendency to take the wrong one.

THE CONSCIOUS SELF AND THE UNCONSCIOUS SELF

In order to understand properly the phenomena of suggestion, or to speak more correctly of autosuggestion, it is necessary to know that two absolutely distinct selves exist within us. Both are intelligent, but while one is conscious the other is unconscious. For this reason the existence of the latter generally escapes notice. It is however easy to prove its existence if one merely takes the trouble to examine certain phenomena and to reflect a few moments upon them.

Let us take for instance the following examples: Every one has heard of somnambulism; every one knows that a somnambulist gets up at night without waking, leaves his room after either dressing himself or not, goes downstairs, walks along corridors, and after having executed certain acts or accomplished certain work, returns to his room, goes to bed again, and shows next day the greatest astonishment at finding work finished which he had left unfinished the day before. It is however he himself who has done it without being aware of it. What force has his body obeyed if it is not an unconscious force, in fact his unconscious self?

Let us now examine the alas, too frequent case of a drunkard attacked by delirium tremens. As though seized with madness he picks up the nearest weapon, knife, hammer, or hatchet, as the case may be, and strikes furiously those who are unlucky enough to be in his vicinity. Once the attack is over, he recovers his senses and contemplates with horror the scene of carnage around him, without realizing that he himself is the author of it. Here again is it not the unconscious self which has caused the unhappy man to act in this way? (And what aversions, what ills we create for ourselves, everyone of us and in every domain by not "immediately" bringing into play "good conscious autosuggestions" against our "bad unconscious autosuggestions," thus bringing about the disappearance of all unjust suffering.)

If we compare the conscious with the unconscious self we see that the conscious self is often possessed of a very unreliable memory while the unconscious self on the contrary is provided with a marvelous and impeccable memory which registers without our knowledge the smallest events, the least important acts of our existence. Further, it is credulous and accepts with unreasoning docility what it is told. [This would suggest that it is our unconscious self that dreams, since in dreams we accept circumstances without question, even when they are absurd. Donald Tyson]

Thus, as it is the unconscious that is responsible for the functioning of all our organs but the intermediary of the brain, a result is produced which may seem rather paradoxical to you: that is, if it believes that a certain organ functions well or ill, or that we feel such and such an impression, the organ in question does indeed function well or ill, or we do feel that impression. Not only does the unconscious self preside over the functions of our organism, but also over all our actions whatever they are. It is this that we call imagination, and it is this which, contrary to accepted opinion, always makes us act, even and above all against our will when there is antagonism between these two forces.

WILL AND IMAGINATION

If we open a dictionary and look up the word "will", we find this definition: "The faculty of freely determining certain acts". We accept this definition as true and unattackable, although nothing could be more false. This "will" that we claim so proudly, always yields to the imagination. It is an absolute rule that admits of no exception. "Blasphemy! Paradox!" you will exclaim. "Not at all! On the contrary, it is the purest truth," I shall reply.

In order to convince yourself of it, open your eyes, look round you and try to understand what you see. You will then come to the conclusion that what I tell you is not an idle theory, offspring of a sick brain but the simple expression of a fact. Suppose that we place on the ground a plank 30 feet long by 1 foot wide. It is evident that everybody will be capable of going from one end to the other of this plank without stepping over the edge. But now change the conditions of the experiment, and imagine this plank placed at the height of the towers of a cathedral. Who then will be capable of advancing even a few feet along this narrow path? Could you hear me speak? Probably not. Before you had taken two steps you would begin to tremble, and in spite of every effort of your will you would be certain to fall to the ground. Why is it then that you would not fall if the plank is on the ground, and why should you fall if it is raised to a height above the ground? Simply because in the first case you imagine that it is easy to go to the end of this plank, while in the second case you imagine that you cannot do so. Notice that your will is powerless to make you advance; if you imagine that you cannot, it is absolutely impossible for you to do so. If tilers and carpenters are able to accomplish this feat, it is because they think they can do it.

Vertigo is entirely caused by the picture we make in our minds that we are going to fall. This picture transforms itself immediately into fact in spite of all the efforts of our will, and the more violent these efforts are, the quicker is the opposite to the desired result brought about. Let us now consider the case of a person suffering from insomnia. If he does not make any effort to sleep, he will lie quietly in bed. If on the contrary he tries to force himself to sleep by his will, the more efforts he makes, the more restless he becomes. Have you not noticed that the more you try to remember the name of a person which you have forgotten, the more it eludes you, until, substituting in your mind the idea "I shall remember in a minute" to the idea "I have forgotten", the name comes back to you of its own accord without the least effort?

Let those of you who are cyclists remember the days when you were learning to ride. You went along clutching the handlebars and frightened of falling. Suddenly catching sight of the smallest obstacle in the road you tried to avoid it, and the more efforts you made to do so, the more surely you rushed upon it. Who has not suffered from an attack of uncontrollable laughter, which bursts out more violently the more one tries to control it? What was the state of mind of each person in these different circumstances? "I do not want to fall but I cannot help doing so"; "I want to sleep but I cannot"; "I want to remember the name of Mrs. So and So, but I cannot"; "I want to avoid the obstacle, but I cannot"; "I want to stop laughing, but I cannot." As you see, in each of these conflicts it is always the imagination which gains the victory over the will, without any exception.

To the same order of ideas belongs the case of the leader who rushes forward at the head of his troops and always carries them along with him, while the cry "Each man for himself!" is almost certain to cause a defeat. Why is this? It is because in the first case the men imagine that they must go forward, and in the second they imagine that they are conquered and must fly for their lives. Panurge was quite aware of the contagion of example, that is to say the action of the imagination, when, to avenge himself upon a merchant on board the same boat, he bought his biggest sheep and threw it into the sea, certain beforehand that the entire flock would follow, which indeed happened.

We human beings have a certain resemblance to sheep, and involuntarily, we are irresistibly impelled to follow other people's examples, imagining that we cannot do otherwise. I could quote a thousand other examples but I should fear to bore you by such an enumeration. I cannot however pass by in silence this fact which shows the enormous power of the imagination, or in other words of the unconscious in its struggle against the will. There are certain drunkards who wish to give up drinking, but who cannot do so. Ask them, and they will reply in all sincerity that they desire to be sober, that drink disgusts them, but that they are irresistibly impelled to drink against their will, in spite of the harm they know it will do them. In the same way certain criminals commit crimes in spite of themselves, and when they are asked why they acted so, they answer: "I could not help it, something impelled me, it was stronger than I." And the drunkard and the criminal speak the truth; they are forced to do what they do, for the simple reason they imagine they cannot prevent themselves from doing so. Thus we who are so proud of our will, who believe that we are free to act as we like, are in reality nothing but wretched puppets of which our imagination holds all the strings. We only cease to be puppets when we have learned to guide our imagination.

SUGGESTION AND AUTOSUGGESTION

According to the preceding remarks we can compare the imagination to a torrent which fatally sweeps away the poor wretch who has fallen into it, in spite of his efforts to gain the bank. This torrent seems indomitable; but if you know how, you can turn it from its course and conduct it to the factory, and there you can transform its force into movement, heat, and electricity.

If this simile is not enough, we may compare the imagination -- "the madman at home" as it has been called -- to an unbroken horse which has neither bridle nor reins. What can the rider do except let himself go wherever the horse wishes to take him? And often if the latter runs away, his mad career only comes to end in the ditch. If, however, the rider succeeds in putting a bridle on the horse, the parts are reversed. It is no longer the horse that goes where he likes; it is the rider who obliges the horse to take him wherever he wishes to go.

Now that we have learned to realize the enormous power of the unconscious or imaginative being, I am going to show how this self, hitherto considered indomitable, can be as easily controlled as a torrent or an unbroken horse. But before going any further it is necessary to define carefully two words that are often used without being properly understood. These are the words suggestion and autosuggestion.

What then is suggestion? It may be defined as "the act of imposing an idea on the brain of another". Does this action really exist? Properly speaking, no. Suggestion does not indeed exist by itself. It does not and cannot exist except on the sine qua non condition of transforming itself into autosuggestion in the subject. This latter word may be defined as "the implanting of an idea in oneself by oneself." You may make a suggestion to someone; if the unconscious of the latter does not accept the suggestion, if it has not, as it were, digested it, in order to transform it into autosuggestion, it produces no result. I have myself occasionally made a more or less commonplace suggestion to ordinarily very obedient subjects quite unsuccessfully. The reason is that the unconscious of the subject refused to accept it and did not transform it into autosuggestion.

THE USE OF AUTOSUGGESTION

Let us now return to the point where I said that we can control and lead our imagination, just as a torrent or an unbroken horse can be controlled. To do so, it is enough in the first place to know that this is possible (of which fact almost everyone is ignorant) and secondly, to know by what means it can be done. Well, the means is very simple; it is that which we have used every day since we came into the world, without wishing or knowing it and absolutely unconsciously, but which unfortunately for us, we often use wrongly and to our own detriment. This means is autosuggestion.

Whereas we constantly give ourselves unconscious autosuggestions, all we have to do is to give ourselves conscious ones, and the process consists in this: first, to weigh carefully in one's mind the things which are to be the object of the autosuggestion, and according as they require the answer "yes" or "no" to repeat several times without thinking of anything else: "This thing is coming", or "this thing is going away"; "this thing will, or will not happen, etc., etc. . . .". (Of course, the thing must be in our power.) If the unconscious accepts this suggestion and transforms it into an autosuggestion, the thing or things are realized in every particular. Thus understood, autosuggestion is nothing but hypnotism as I see it, and I would define it in these simple words: The influence of the imagination upon the moral and physical being of mankind.

Now this influence is undeniable, and without returning to previous examples, I will quote a few others. If you persuade yourself that you can do a certain thing, provided this thing be possible, you will do it however difficult it may be. If on the contrary you imagine that you cannot do the simplest thing in the world, it is impossible for you to do it, and molehills become for you unscalable mountains. Such is the case of neurasthenics, who, believing themselves incapable of the least effort, often find it impossible even to walk a few steps without being exhausted. And these same neurasthenics sink more deeply into their depression, the more efforts they make to throw it off, like the poor wretch in the quicksands who sinks in all the deeper the more he tries to struggle out. In the same way it is sufficient to think a pain is going, to feel it indeed disappear little by little, and inversely, it is enough to think that one suffers in order to feel the pain begin to come immediately.

I know certain people who predict in advance that they will have a sick headache on a certain day, in certain circumstances, and on that day, in the given circumstances, sure enough, they feel it. They brought their illness on themselves, just as others cure theirs by conscious autosuggestion. I know that one generally passes for mad in the eyes of the world if one dares to put forward ideas which it is not accustomed to hear. Well, at the risk of being thought so, I say that if certain people are ill mentally and physically, it is that they imagine themselves to be ill mentally or physically. If certain others are paralytic without having any lesion to account for it, it is that they imagine themselves to be paralyzed, and it is among such persons that the most extraordinary cures are produced. If others again are happy or unhappy, it is that they imagine themselves to be so, for it is possible for two people in exactly the same circumstances to be, the one perfectly happy, the other absolutely wretched.

Neurasthenia, stammering, aversions, kleptomania, certain cases of paralysis, are nothing but the result of unconscious autosuggestion, that is to say the result of the action of the unconscious upon the physical and moral being. But if our unconscious is the source of many of our ills, it can also bring about the cure of our physical and mental ailments. It can not only repair the ill it has done, but cure real illnesses, so strong is its action upon our organism. Shut yourself up alone in a room, seat yourself in an armchair, close your eyes to avoid any distraction, and concentrate your mind for a few moments on thinking: "Such and such a thing is going to disappear", or "Such and such a thing is coming to pass."

If you have really made the autosuggestion, that is to say, if your unconscious has assimilated the idea that you have presented to it, you are astonished to see the thing you have thought come to pass. (Note that it is the property of ideas autosuggested to exist within us unrecognized, and we can only know of their existence by the effect they produce.) But above all, and this is an essential point, the will must not be brought into play in practising autosuggestion; for, if it is not in agreement with the imagination, if one thinks: "I will make such and such a thing happen", and the imagination says: "You are willing it, but it is not going to be", not only does one not obtain what one wants, but even exactly the reverse is brought about. This remark is of capital importance, and explains why results are so unsatisfactory when, in treating moral ailments, one strives to re-educate the will. It is the training of the imagination which is necessary, and it is thanks to this shade of difference that my method has often succeeded where others --and those not the least considered -- have failed. From the numerous experiments that I have made daily for twenty years, and which I have examined with minute care, I have been able to deduct the following conclusions which I have summed up as laws:

1   When the will and the imagination are antagonistic, it is always the imagination which wins, without any exception.

2   In the conflict between the will and the imagination, the force of the imagination is in direct ratio to the square of the will.

3   When the will and the imagination are in agreement, one does not add to the other, but one is multiplied by the other.

4   The imagination can be directed. (The expressions "In direct ratio to the square of the

will" and "Is multiplied by" are not rigorously exact. They are simply illustrations destined to make my meaning clearer.)

After what has just been said it would seem that nobody ought to be ill. That is quite true. Every illness, whatever it may be, can yield to autosuggestion.

Daring and unlikely as my statement may seem, I do not say does always yield, but can yield, which is a different thing. But in order to lead people to practise conscious autosuggestion they must be taught how, just as they are taught to read or write or play the piano. Autosuggestion is, as I said above, an instrument that we possess at birth, and with which we play unconsciously all our life, as a baby plays with its rattle. It is however a dangerous instrument; it can wound or even kill you if you handle it imprudently and unconsciously. It can on the contrary save your life when you know how to employ it consciously. One can say of it as Aesop said of the tongue: "It is at the same time the best and the worst thing in the world".

I am now going to show you how everyone can profit by the beneficent action of autosuggestion consciously applied. In saying "every one", I exaggerate a little, for there are two classes of persons in whom it is difficult to arouse conscious autosuggestion:

1   The mentally undeveloped who are not capable of understanding what you say to them.

2   Those who are unwilling to understand.

HOW TO TEACH PATIENTS TO MAKE AUTOSUGGESTIONS

The principle of the method may be summed up in these few words: It is impossible to think of two things at once; that is to say that two ideas may be in juxtaposition, but they cannot be superimposed in our mind. Every thought entirely filling our mind becomes true for us and tends to transform itself into action. Thus if you can make a sick person think that her trouble is getting better, it will disappear; if you succeed in making a kleptomaniac think that he will not steal any more, he will cease to steal, etc., etc. This training which perhaps seems to you an impossibility, is, however, the simplest thing in the world. It is enough, by a series of appropriate and graduated experiments, to teach the subject, as it were the A. B. C. of conscious thought, and here is the series: by following it to the letter one can be absolutely sure of obtaining a good result, except with the two categories of persons mentioned above.

First experiment. (These experiments are those of Sage of Rochester.)

Preparatory. -- Ask the subject to stand upright, with the body as stiff as an iron bar, the feet close together from toe to heel, while keeping the ankles flexible as if they were hinges. Tell him to make himself like a plank with hinges at its base, which is balanced on the ground. Make him notice that if one pushes the plank slightly either way it falls as a mass without any resistance, in the direction in which it is pushed. Tell him that you are going to pull him back by the shoulders and that he must let himself fall in your arms without the slightest resistance, turning on his ankles as on hinges, that is to say keeping the feet fixed to the ground. Then pull him back by the shoulders and if the experiment does not succeed, repeat it until it does, or nearly so.

Second experiment. -- Begin by explaining to the subject that in order to demonstrate the action of the imagination upon us, you are going to ask him in a moment to think: "I am falling backwards, I am falling backwards . . ." Tell him that he must have no thought but this in his mind, that he must not reflect or wonder if he is going to fall or not, or think that if he falls he may hurt himself, etc., or fall back purposely to please you, but that if he really feels something impelling him to fall backwards, he must not resist but obey the impulse. Then ask your subject to raise the head high and to shut his eyes, and place your right fist on the back of his neck, and your left hand on his forehead, and say to him: "Now think: I am falling backwards, I am falling backwards, etc., etc. . . " and, indeed, "You are falling backwards, You . . . are. . . fall . . . ing . . . back . . . wards, etc." At the same time slide the left hand lightly backwards to the left temple, above the ear, and remove very slowly but with a continuous movement the right fist. The subject is immediately felt to make a slight movement backwards, and either to stop himself from falling or else to fall completely. In the first case, tell him that he has resisted, and that he did not think just that he was falling, but that he might hurt himself if he did fall. That is true, for if he had not thought the latter, he would have fallen like a block. Repeat the experiment using a tone of command as if you would force the subject to obey you. Go on with it until it is completely successful or very nearly so. The operator should stand a little behind the subject, the left leg forward and the right leg well behind him, so as not to be knocked over by the subject when he falls. Neglect of this precaution might result in a double fall if the person is heavy.

Third experiment. -- Place the subject facing you, the body still stiff, the ankles flexible, and the feet joined and parallel. Put your two hands on his temples without any pressure, look fixedly, without moving the eyelids, at the root of his nose, and tell him to think: "I am falling forward, I am falling forward . . . " and repeat to him, stressing the syllables, "You are fall . . . ing . . . for . . . ward, You are fall . . . ing . . . for . . . ward . . ." without ceasing to look fixedly at him.

Fourth experiment. -- Ask the subject to clasp his hands as tight as possible, that is to say, until the fingers tremble slightly, look at him in the same way as in the preceding experiment and keep your hands on his as though to squeeze them together still more tightly. Tell him to think that he cannot unclasp his fingers, that you are going to count three, and that when you say "three" he is to try to separate his hands while thinking all the time: "I cannot do it, I cannot do it . . . " and he will find it impossible. Then count very slowly, "one, two, three", and add immediately, detaching the syllables: "You . . . can . . . not . . . do . . . it . . . .

You . . . can . . . not . . . do . . . it . . ." If the subject is thinking properly, "I cannot do it", not only is he unable to separate his fingers, but the latter clasp themselves all the more tightly together the more efforts he makes to separate them. He obtains in fact exactly the contrary to what he wants. In a few moments say to him: "Now think: 'I can do it,'" and his fingers will separate themselves. Be careful always to keep your eyes fixed on the root of the subject's nose, and do not allow him to turn his eyes away from yours for a single moment. If he is able to unclasp his hands, do not think it is your own fault, it is the subject's; he has not properly thought: "I cannot". Assure him firmly of this, and begin the experiment again. Always use a tone of command which suffers no disobedience. I do not mean that it is necessary to raise your voice; on the contrary it is preferable to employ the ordinary pitch, but stress every word in a dry and imperative tone.

When these experiments have been successful, all the others succeed equally well and can be easily obtained by carrying out to the letter the instructions given above. Some subjects are very sensitive, and it is easy to recognize them by the fact that the contraction of their fingers and limbs is easily produced. After two or three successful experiments, it is no longer necessary to say to them: "Think this", or "think that"; You need only, for example, say to them simply -- but in the imperative tone employed by all good suggestionists -- "Close your hands; now you cannot open them". "Shut your eyes; now you cannot open them," and the subject finds it absolutely impossible to open the hands or the eyes in spite of all his efforts. Tell him in a few moments: "You can do it now," and the de-contraction takes place instantaneously. These experiments can be varied to infinity.

Here are a few more: Make the subject join his hands, and suggest that they are welded together; make him put his hand on the table, and suggest that it is stuck to it; tell him that he is fixed to his chair and cannot rise; make him rise, and tell him he cannot walk; put a penholder on the table and tell him that it weighs a hundredweight, and that he cannot lift it, etc., etc. In all these experiments, I cannot repeat too often, it is not suggestion properly so-called which produces the phenomena, but the autosuggestion which is consecutive to the suggestion of the operator.

METHOD OF PROCEDURE IN CURATIVE SUGGESTION

When the subject has passed through the preceding experiments and has understood them, he is ripe for curative suggestion. He is like a cultivated field in which the seed can germinate and develop, whereas before it was but rough earth in which it would have perished. Whatever ailment the subject suffers from, whether it is physical or mental, it is important to proceed always in the same way, and to use the same words with a few variations according to the case. Say to the subject: "Sit down and close your eyes. I am not going to try and put you to sleep as it is quite unnecessary. I ask you to close your eyes simply in order that your attention may not be distracted by the objects around you. Now tell yourself that every word I say is going to fix itself in your mind, and be printed, engraved, and encrusted in it; that there, it is going to stay fixed, imprinted, and encrusted, and that without your will or knowledge, in fact perfectly unconsciously on your part, you yourself and your whole organism are going to obey."

In the first place I say: "Every day, three times a day, in the morning, at midday, and in the evening, at the usual meal times, you will feel hungry, that is to say, you will experience the agreeable sensation which makes you think and say: "Oh! How nice it will be to have something to eat!" You will then eat and enjoy your food, without of course overeating. You will also be careful to masticate it properly so as to transform it into a sort of soft paste before swallowing it. In these conditions you will digest it properly, and so feel no discomfort, inconvenience, or pain of any kind either in the stomach or intestines. You will assimilate what you eat and your organism will make use of it to make blood, muscle, strength and energy, in a word: Life.

"Since you will have digested your food properly, the function of excretion will be normal, and every morning, on rising, you will feel the need of evacuating the bowels, and without ever being obliged to take medicine or to use any artifice, you will obtain a normal and satisfactory result.

"Further, every night from the time you wish to go to sleep till the time you wish to wake next morning, you will sleep deeply, calmly, and quietly, without nightmares, and on waking you will feel perfectly well, cheerful, and active.

"Likewise, if you occasionally suffer from depression, if you are gloomy and prone to worry and look on the dark side of things, from now onwards you will cease to do so, and, instead of worrying and being depressed and looking on the dark side of things, you are going to feel perfectly cheerful, possibly without any special reason for it, just as you used to feel depressed for no particular reason. I say further still, that even if you have real reason to be worried and depressed you are not going to be so.

"If you are also subject to occasional fits of impatience or ill-temper you will cease to have them: on the contrary you will be always patient and master of yourself, and the things which worried, annoyed, or irritated you, will henceforth leave you absolutely indifferent and perfectly calm.

"If you are sometimes attacked, pursued, haunted, by bad and unwholesome ideas, by apprehensions, fears, aversions, temptations, or grudges against other people, all that will be gradually lost sight of by your imagination, and will melt away and lose itself as though in a distant cloud where it will finally disappear completely. As a dream vanishes when we wake, so will all these vain images disappear.

"To this I add that all your organs are performing their functions properly. The heart beats in a normal way and the circulation of the blood takes place as it should; the lungs are carrying out their functions, as also the stomach, the intestines, the liver, the biliary duct, the kidneys and the bladder. If at the present moment any of them is acting abnormally, that abnormality is becoming less every day, so that quite soon it will have vanished completely, and the organ will have recovered its normal function. Further, if there should be any lesions in any of these organs, they will get better from day to day and will soon be entirely healed." (With regard to this, I may say that it is not necessary to know which organ is affected for it to be cured. Under the influence of the autosuggestion "Every day, in every respect, I am getting better and better", the unconscious acts upon the organ which it can pick out itself.)

"I must also add --and it is extremely important -- that if up to the present you have lacked confidence in yourself, I tell you that this self-distrust will disappear little by little and give place to self-confidence, based on the knowledge of this force of incalculable power which is in each one of us. It is absolutely necessary for every human being to have this confidence. Without it one can accomplish nothing, with it one can accomplish whatever one likes, (within reason, of course). You are then going to have confidence in yourself, and this confidence gives you the assurance that you are capable of accomplishing perfectly well whatever you wish to do, --on condition that it is reasonable, -- and whatever it is your duty to do.

"So when you wish to do something reasonable, or when you have a duty to perform, always think that it is easy, and make the words difficult, impossible, I cannot, it is stronger than I, I cannot prevent myself from . . . disappear from your vocabulary; they are not English. What is English is: "It is easy and I can". By considering the thing easy it becomes so for you, although it might seem difficult to others. You will do it quickly and well, and without fatigue, because you do it without effort, whereas if you had considered it as difficult or impossible it would have become so for you, simply because you would have thought it so."

To these general suggestions which will perhaps seem long and even childish to some of you, but which are necessary, must be added those which apply to the particular case of the patient you are dealing with. All these suggestions must be made in a monotonous and soothing voice (always emphasizing the essential words), which although it does not actually send the subject to sleep, at least makes him feel drowsy, and think of nothing in particular. When you have come to the end of the series of suggestions you address the subject in these terms: "In short, I mean that from every point of view, physical as well as mental, you are going to enjoy excellent health, better health than that you have been able to enjoy up to the present. Now I am going to count three, and when I say 'Three', you will open your eyes and come out of the passive state in which you are now. You will come out of it quite naturally, without feeling in the least drowsy or tired; on the contrary, you will feel strong, vigorous, alert, active, full of life; further still, you will feel very cheerful and fit in every way. ONE -- TWO -- THREE --"

At the word "three" the subject opens his eyes, always with a smile and an expression of well-being and contentment on his face. Sometimes, -- though rarely, -- the patient is cured on the spot; at other times, and this is more generally the case, he finds himself relieved, his pain or his depression has partially or totally disappeared, though only for a certain lapse of time. In every case it is necessary to renew the suggestions more or less frequently according to your subject, being careful always to space them out at longer and longer intervals, according to the progress obtained until they are no longer necessary, -- that is to say when the cure is complete.

Before sending away your patient, you must tell him that he carries within him the instrument by which he can cure himself, and that you are, as it were, only a professor teaching him to use this instrument, and that he must help you in your task.

Thus, every morning before rising, and every night on getting into bed, he must shut his eyes and in thought transport himself into your presence, and then repeat twenty times consecutively in a monotonous voice, counting by means of a string with twenty knots in it, this little phrase:

"EVERY DAY, IN EVERY RESPECT, I AM GETTING BETTER AND BETTER"

In his mind he should emphasize the words "in every respect" which applies to every need, mental or physical. This general suggestion is more efficacious than special ones. Thus it is easy to realize the part played by the giver of the suggestions. He is not a master who gives orders, but a friend, a guide, who leads the patient step by step on the road to health. As all the suggestions are given in the interest of the patient, the unconscious of the latter asks nothing better than to assimilate them and transform them into autosuggestions. When this has been done, the cure is obtained more or less rapidly according to circumstances.

THE SUPERIORITY OF THIS METHOD

This method gives absolutely marvelous results, and it is easy to understand why. Indeed, by following out my advice, it is impossible to fail, except with the two classes of persons mentioned above, who fortunately represent barely 3 per cent of the whole. If, however, you try to put your subjects to sleep right away, without the explanations and preliminary experiments necessary to bring them to accept the suggestions and to transform them into autosuggestions, you cannot and will not succeed except with peculiarly sensitive subjects, and these are rare. Everybody may become so by training, but very few are so sufficiently without the preliminary instruction that I recommend, which can be done in a few minutes.

Formerly, imagining that suggestions could only be given during sleep, I always tried to put my patient to sleep; but on discovering that it was not indispensable, I left off doing it in order to spare him the dread and uneasiness he almost always experiences when he is told that he is going to be sent to sleep, and which often makes him offer, in spite of himself, an involuntary resistance. If, on the contrary, you tell him that you are not going to put him to sleep as there is no need to do so, you gain his confidence. He listens to you without fear or any ulterior thought, and it often happens -- if not the first time, anyhow very soon -- that, soothed by the monotonous sound of your voice, he falls into a deep sleep from which he awakes astonished at having slept at all. If there are sceptics among you -- as I am quite sure there are -- all I have to say to them is: "Come to my house and see what is being done, and you will be convinced by fact."

You must not however run away with the idea that autosuggestion can only be brought about in the way I have described. It is possible to make suggestions to people without their knowledge and without any preparation. For instance, if a doctor who by his title alone has a suggestive influence on his patient, tells him that he can do nothing for him, and that his illness is incurable, he provokes in the mind of the latter an autosuggestion which may have the most disastrous consequences; if however he tells him that his illness is a serious one, it is true, but that with care, time, and patience, he can be cured, he sometimes and even often obtains results which will surprise him.

Here is another example: if a doctor after examining his patient, writes a prescription and gives it to him without any comment, the remedies prescribed will not have much chance of succeeding; if, on the other hand, he explains to his patient that such and such medicines must be taken in such and such conditions and that they will produce certain results, those results are practically certain to be brought about.

If in this hall there are medical men or brother chemists, I hope they will not think me their enemy. I am on the contrary their best friend. On the one hand I should like to see the theoretical and practical study of suggestion on the syllabus of the medical schools for the great benefit of the sick and of the doctors themselves; and on the other hand, in my opinion, every time that a patient goes to see his doctor, the latter should order him one or even several medicines, even if they are not necessary. As a matter of fact, when a patient visits his doctor, it is in order to be told what medicine will cure him. He does not realize that it is the hygiene and regimen which do this, and he attaches little importance to them. It is a medicine that he wants.

In my opinion, if the doctor only prescribes a regimen without any medicine, his patient will be dissatisfied; he will say that he took the trouble to consult him for nothing, and often goes to another doctor. It seems to me then that the doctor should always prescribe medicines to his patient, and, as much as possible, medicines made up by himself rather than the standard remedies so much advertised and which owe their only value to the advertisement. The doctor's own prescriptions will inspire infinitely more confidence than So and So's pills which anyone can procure easily at the nearest drug store without any need of a prescription.

HOW SUGGESTION WORKS

In order to understand properly the part played by suggestion or rather by autosuggestion, it is enough to know that the unconscious self is the grand director of all our functions. Make this believed, as I said above, that a certain organ which does not function well must perform its function, and instantly the order is transmitted. The organ obeys with docility, and either at once or little by little performs its functions in a normal manner. This explains simply and clearly how by means of suggestion one can stop haemorrhages, cure constipation, cause fibrous tumours to disappear, cure paralysis, tubercular lesions, varicose; ulcers, etc.

Let us take for example, a case of dental haemorrhage which I had the opportunity of observing in the consulting room of M. Gauthe, a dentist at Troyes. A young lady whom I had helped to cure herself of asthma from which she had suffered for eight years, told me one day that she wanted to have a tooth out. As I knew her to be very sensitive, I offered to make her feel nothing of the operation. She naturally accepted with pleasure and we made an appointment with the dentist. On the day we had arranged we presented ourselves at the dentist's and, standing opposite my patient, I looked fixedly at her, saying: "You feel nothing, you feel nothing, etc., etc." and then while still continuing the suggestion I made a sign to the dentist. In an instant the tooth was out without Mlle. D_____ turning a hair.

As fairly often happens, a haemorrhage followed, but I told the dentist that I would try suggestion without his using a haemostatic, without knowing beforehand what would happen. I then asked Mile. D_____ to look at me fixedly, and I suggested to her that in two minutes the haemorrhage would cease of its own accord, and we waited. The patient spat blood again once or twice, and then ceased. I told her to open her mouth, and we both looked and found that a clot of blood had formed in the dental cavity. How is this phenomenon to be explained? In the simplest way. Under the influence of the idea: "The haemorrhage is to stop", the unconscious had sent to the small arteries and veins the order to stop the flow of blood, and, obediently, they contracted naturally, as they would have done artificially at the contact of a haemostatic like adrenalin, for example. The same reasoning explains how a fibrous tumour can be made to disappear. The unconscious having accepted the idea "It is to go", the brain orders the arteries which nourish it to contract. They do so, refusing their services, and ceasing to nourish the tumour which, deprived of nourishment, dies, dries up, is reabsorbed and disappears.

THE USE OF SUGGESTION FOR THE CURE OF MORAL AILMENTS AND TAINTS EITHER CONGENITAL OR ACQUIRED

Neurasthenia, so common nowadays, generally yields to suggestion constantly practised in the way I have indicated. I have had the happiness of contributing to the cure of a large number of neurasthenics with whom every other treatment had failed. One of them had even spent a month in a special establishment at Luxemburg without obtaining any improvement. In six weeks he was completely cured, and he is now the happiest man one would wish to find, after having thought himself the most miserable. Neither is he ever likely to fall ill again in the same way, for I showed him how to make use of conscious autosuggestion and he does it marvelously well.

But if suggestion is useful in treating moral complaints and physical ailments, may it not render still greater services to society, in turning into honest folks the wretched children who people our reformatories and who only leave them to enter the army of crime? Let no one tell me it is impossible. The remedy exists and I can prove it. I will quote the two following cases which are very characteristic, but here I must insert a few remarks in parenthesis. To make you understand the way in which suggestion acts in the treatment of moral taints I will use the following comparison. Suppose our brain is a plank in which are driven nails which represent the ideas, habits, and instincts, which determine our actions. If we find that there exists in a subject a bad idea, a bad habit, a bad instinct, -- as it were, a bad nail, we take another which is the good idea, habit, or instinct, place it on top of the bad one and give a tap with a hammer -- in other words we make a suggestion. The new nail will be driven in perhaps a fraction of an inch, while the old one will come out to the same extent. At each fresh blow with the hammer, that is to say at each fresh suggestion, the one will be driven in a fraction further and the other will be driven out the same amount, until, after a certain number of blows, the old nail will come out completely and be replaced by the new one. When this substitution has been made, the individual obeys it.

Let us return to our examples. Little M_____, a child of eleven living at Troyes, was subject night and day to certain accidents inherent to early infancy [bed-wetting]. He was also a kleptomaniac, and, of course, untruthful into the bargain. At his mother's request I treated him by suggestion. After the first visit the accidents ceased by day, but continued at night. Little by little they became less frequent, and finally, a few months afterwards, the child was completely cured. In the same period his thieving propensities lessened, and in six months they had entirely ceased.

This child's brother, aged eighteen, had conceived a violent hatred against another of his brothers. Every time that he had taken a little too much wine, he felt impelled to draw a knife and stab his brother. He felt that one day or other he would end by doing so, and he knew at the same time that having done so he would be inconsolable. I treated him also by suggestion, and the result was marvelous. After the first treatment he was cured. His hatred for his brother had disappeared, and they have since become good friends and got on capitally together. I followed up the case for a long time, and the cure was permanent.

Since such results are to be obtained by suggestion, would it not be beneficial -- I might even say indispensable -- to take up this method and introduce it into our reformatories? I am absolutely convinced that if suggestion were daily applied to vicious children, more than 50 per cent could be reclaimed. Would it not be an immense service to render society, to bring back to it sane and well members of it who were formerly corroded by moral decay? Perhaps I shall be told that suggestion is a dangerous thing, and that it can be used for evil purposes. This is no valid objection, first because the practice of suggestion would only be confided [by the patient] to reliable and honest people, -- to the reformatory doctors, for instance, -- and on the other hand, those who seek to use it for evil ask no one's permission.

But even admitting that it offers some danger (which is not so) I should like to ask whoever proffers the objection, to tell me what thing we use that is not dangerous? Is it steam? gunpowder? railways? ships? electricity? automobiles? aeroplanes? Are the poisons not dangerous which we, doctors and chemists, use daily in minute doses, and which might easily destroy the patient if, in a moment's carelessness, we unfortunately made a mistake in weighing them out?

A FEW TYPICAL CURES

This little work would be incomplete if it did not include a few examples of the cures obtained. It would take too long, and would also perhaps be somewhat tiring if I were to relate all those in which I have taken part. I will therefore content myself by quoting a few of the most remarkable.

Mlle. M_____ D_____, of Troyes, had suffered for eight years from asthma which obliged her to sit up in bed nearly all night, fighting for breath. Preliminary experiments show that she is a very sensitive subject. She sleeps immediately, and the suggestion is given. From the first treatment there is an enormous improvement. The patient has a good night, only interrupted by one attack of asthma which only lasts a quarter of an hour. In a very short time the asthma disappears completely and there is no relapse later on.

M. M_____, a working hosier living at Sainte-Savine near Troyes, paralyzed for two years as the result of injuries at the junction of the spinal column and the pelvis. The paralysis is only in the lower limbs, in which the circulation of the blood has practically ceased, making them swollen, congested, and discolored. Several treatments, including the antisyphilitic, have been tried without success. Preliminary experiments successful; suggestion applied by me, and autosuggestion by the patient for eight days. At the end of this time there is an almost imperceptible but still appreciable movement of the left leg. Renewed suggestion. In eight days the improvement is noticeable. Every week or fortnight there is an increased improvement with progressive lessening of the swelling, and so on. Eleven months afterwards, on the first of November, 1906, the patient goes downstairs alone and walks 800 yards, and in the month of July, 1907, goes back to the factory where he has continued to work since that time, with no trace of paralysis.

M. A_____ G_____, living at Troyes, has long suffered from enteritis, for which different treatments have been tried in vain. He is also in a very bad state mentally, being depressed, gloomy, unsociable, and obsessed by thoughts of suicide. Preliminary experiments easy, followed by suggestion which produces an appreciable result from the very day. For three months, daily suggestions to begin with, then at increasingly longer intervals. At the end of this time, the cure is complete, the enteritis has disappeared, and his morals have become excellent. As the cure dates back twelve years without the shadow of a relapse, it may be considered as permanent.

M. G_____, is a striking example of the effects that can be produced by suggestion, or rather by autosuggestion. At the same time as I made suggestions to him from the physical point of view, I also did so from the mental, and he accepted both suggestions equally well. Every day his confidence in himself increased, and as he was an excellent workman, in order to earn more, he looked out for a machine which would enable him to work at home for his employer. A little later a factory owner having seen with his own eyes what a good workman he was, entrusted him with the very machine he desired. Thanks to his skill he was able to turn out much more than an ordinary workman, and his employer, delighted with the result, gave him another and yet another machine, until M. G, who, but for suggestion, would have remained an ordinary workman, is now in charge of six machines which bring him a very hand some profit.

Mme. D_____, at Troyes, about 30 years of age. She is in the last stages of consumption, and grows thinner daily in spite of special nourishment. She suffers from coughing and spitting, and has difficulty in breathing; in fact, from all appearances she has only a few months to live. Preliminary experiments show great sensitiveness, and suggestion is followed by immediate improvement. From the next day the morbid symptoms begin to lessen. Every day the improvement becomes more marked, the patient rapidly puts on flesh, although she no longer takes special nourishment. In a few months tbe cure is apparently complete. This person wrote to me on the 1st of January, 1911, that is to say eight months after I had left Troyes, to thank me and to tell me that, although pregnant, she was perfectly well.

I have purposely chosen these cases dating some time back, in order to show that the cures are permanent, but I should like to add a few more recent ones.

M. X_____, Post Office clerk at Luneville. Having lost one of his children in January, 1910, the trouble produces in him a cerebral disturbance which manifests itself by uncontrollable nervous trembling. His uncle brings him to me in the month of June. Preliminary experiments followed by suggestion. Four days afterwards the patient returns to tell me that the trembling has disappeared. I renew the suggestion and tell him to return in eight days. A week, then a fortnight, then three weeks, then a month, pass by without my hearing any more of him. Shortly afterwards his uncle comes and tells me that he has just had a letter from his nephew, who is perfectly well. He has taken on again his work as telegraphist which he had been obliged to give up, and the day before, he had sent off a telegram of 170 words without the least difficulty. He could easily, he added in his letter, have sent off an even longer one. Since then he has had no relapse.

M. Y_____, of Nancy, has suffered from neurasthenia for several years. He has aversions, nervous fears, and disorders of the stomach and intestines. He sleeps badly, is gloomy and is haunted by ideas of suicide; he staggers when he walks like a drunken man, and can think of nothing but his trouble. All treatments have failed and he gets worse and worse; a stay in a special nursing home for such cases has no effect whatever. M. Y_____ comes to see me at the beginning of October, 1910. Preliminary experiments comparatively easy. I explain to the patient the principles of autosuggestion, and the existence within us of the conscious and the unconscious self, and then make the required suggestion. For two or three days M. Y_____ has a little difficulty with the explanations I have given him. In a short time light breaks in upon his mind, and he grasps the whole thing. I renew the suggestion, and he makes it himself too every day. The improvement, which is at first slow, becomes more and more rapid, and in a month and a half the cure is complete. The ex-invalid who had lately considered himself the most wretched of men, now thinks himself the happiest.

M. E_____, of Troyes. An attack of gout; the right ankle is inflamed and painful, and he is unable to walk. The preliminary experiments show him to be a very sensitive subject. After the first treatment he is able to regain, without the help of his stick, the carriage which brought him, and the pain has ceased. The next day he does not return as I had told him to do. Afterwards his wife comes alone and tells me that that morning her husband had got up, put on his shoes, and gone off on his bicycle to visit his yards (he is a painter). It is needless to tell you my utter astonishment. I was not able to follow up this case, as the patient never deigned to come and see me again, but some time afterward I heard that he had had no relapse.

Mme. T_____, of Nancy. Neurasthenia, dyspepsia, gastralgia, enteritis, and pains in different parts of the body. She has treated herself for several years with a negative result. I treat her by suggestion, and she makes autosuggestions for herself every day. From the first day there is a noticeable improvement which continues without interruption. At the present moment this person has long been cured mentally and physically, and follows no regimen. She thinks that she still has perhaps a slight touch of enteritis, but she is not sure.

Mme. X_____, a sister of Mme. T_____. Acute neurasthenia; she stays in bed a fortnight every month, as it is totally impossible for her to move or work; she suffers from lack of appetite, depression, and digestive disorders. She is cured by one visit, and the cure seems to be permanent as she has had no relapse.

Mme. H_____, at Maxeville. General eczema, which is particularly severe on the left leg. Both legs are inflamed, above all at the ankles; walking is difficult and painful. I treat her by suggestion. That same evening Mme. H_____ is able to walk several hundred yards without fatigue. The day after the feet and ankles are no longer swollen and have not been swollen again since. The eczema disappears rapidly.

Mme. F_____, at Laneuveville. Pains in the kidneys and the knees. The illness dates from ten years back and is becoming worse every day. Suggestion from me, and autosuggestion from herself. The improvement is immediate and increases progressively. The cure is obtained rapidly, and is a permanent one.

Mme. Z_____, of Nancy, felt ill in January, 1910, with congestion of the lungs, from which she had not recovered two months later. She suffers from general weakness, loss of appetite, bad digestive trouble, rare and difficult bowel action, insomnia, copious night-sweats. After the first suggestion, the patient feels much better, and two days later she returns and tells me that she feels quite well. Every trace of illness has disappeared, and all the organs are functioning normally. Three or four times she had been on the point of sweating, but each time prevented it by the use of conscious autosuggestion. From this time Mme. Z_____ has enjoyed perfectly good health.

M. X_____, at Belfort, cannot talk for more than ten minutes or a quarter of an hour without becoming completely aphonous. Different doctors consulted find no lesion in the vocal organs, but one of them says that M. X_____ suffers from senility of the larynx, and this conclusion confirms him in the belief that he is incurable. He comes to spend his holidays at Nancy, and a lady of my acquaintance advises him to come and see me. He refuses at first, but eventually consents in spite of his absolute disbelief in the effects of suggestion. I treat him in this way nevertheless, and ask him to return two days afterwards. He comes back on the appointed day, and tells me that the day before he was able to converse the whole afternoon without becoming aphonous. Two days later he returns again to say that his trouble had not reappeared, although he had not only conversed a great deal but even sung the day before. The cure still holds good and I am convinced that it will always do so.

Before closing, I should like to say a few words on the application of my method to the training and correction of children by their parents.

The latter should wait until the child is asleep, and then one of them should enter his room with precaution, stop a yard from his bed, and repeat 15 or 20 times in a murmur all the things they wish to obtain from the child, from the point of view of health, work, sleep, application, conduct, etc. He should then retire as he came, taking great care not to awake the child. This extremely simple process gives the best possible results, and it is easy to understand why. When the child is asleep his body and his conscious self are at rest and, as it were, annihilated; his unconscious self however is awake; it is then to the latter alone that one speaks, and as it is very credulous it accepts what one says to it without dispute, so that, little by little, the child arrives at making of himself what his parents desire him to be.

CONCLUSION

What conclusion is to be drawn from all this? The conclusion is very simple and can be expressed in a few words: We possess within us a force of incalculable power, which, when we handle it unconsciously is often prejudicial to us. If on the contrary we direct it in a conscious and wise manner, it gives us the mastery of ourselves and allows us not only to escape and to aid others to escape, from physical and mental ills, but also to live in relative happiness, whatever the conditions in which we may find ourselves. Lastly, and above all, it should be applied to the moral regeneration of those who have wandered from the right path.

EMILE COUE.

We suggest you now read the book,

"Automatic Wealth, the Secrets of the Millionaire Mind" - Including: As a Man Thinketh, the Science of Getting Rich, the Way to Wealth & Think and Grow Rich [UNABRIDGED] (Paperback)

by Napoleon Hill, James Allen, Wallace D. Wattles, Benjamin Franklin, carefully.

We hope that after you have the opportunity to practice the principles involved in these lessons, you will write to us and let us know of the results in your life.

BN Publishing

Improving People's Life

info@bnpublishing.com

www.bnpublishing.com

We Have Book Recommendations for You

The Strangest Secret by Earl Nightingale   (Audio CD - Jan 2006)

Acres of Diamonds [MP3 AUDIO] [UNABRIDGED] (Audio CD) by Russell H. Conwell

Automatic Wealth: The Secrets of the Millionaire Mind - Including: Acres of Diamonds, As a Man Thinketh, I Dare you!, The Science of Getting Rich, The Way to Wealth, and Think and Grow Rich [UNABRIDGED] by Napoleon Hill, et al (CD-ROM)

Think and Grow Rich [MP3 AUDIO] [UNABRIDGED] by Napoleon Hill, Jason McCoy (Narrator) (Audio CD - January 30, 2006)

As a Man Thinketh [UNABRIDGED]
by James Allen, Jason McCoy (Narrator) (Audio CD)

Your Invisible Power: How to Attain Your Desires by
Letting Your Subconscious Mind Work for You [MP3
AUDIO] [UNABRIDGED]

Thought Vibration or the Law of Attraction in the
Thought World [MP3 AUDIO] [UNABRIDGED]
by William Walker Atkinson, Jason McCoy (Narrator)
(Audio CD - July 1, 2005)

The Law of Success Volume I: The Principles of Self-
Mastery by Napoleon Hill (Audio CD - Feb 21, 2006)

The Law of Success, Volume I: The Principles of Self-
Mastery (Law of Success, Vol. 1) (The Law of Success)
by Napoleon Hill (Paperback - Jun 20, 2006)

The Law of Success, Volumes II & III: A Definite Chief
Aim & Self -Confidence by Napoleon Hill (Paperback -
Jun 20, 2006)

Thought Vibration or the Law of Attraction in the
Thought World & Your Invisible Power (Paperback)

Automatic Wealth, The Secrets of the Millionaire Mind
- Including: As a Man Thinketh, The Science of Getting
Rich, The Way to Wealth and Think and Grow Rich
(Paperback)

The Bestsellers in this Book give sound advice about
money and how to obtain it. Just reach for the stars,
stay focused on your dreams, and watch them come
true. There is nothing we can imagine that we can't do.
So what are we waiting for? Let's begin the journey of
self-fulfillment.

4 Bestsellers in 1 Book:

As a Man Thinketh by James Allen

The Science of Getting Rich by Wallace D. Wattles

The Way to Wealth by Benjamin Franklin

Think and Grow Rich by Napoleon Hill

BN Publishing

Improving People's Life

www.bnpublishing.com